Balboa Press books may be ordered through booksellers or by contacting:

Balboa Press
A Division of Hay House
1663 Liberty Drive
Bloomington, IN 47403
www.balboapress.com
1 (877) 407-4847

ISBN: 978-1-9822-3927-5 (sc)
978-1-9822-3926-8 (e)

Library of Congress Control Number: 2019919501

Print information available on the last page.

Balboa Press rev. date: 12/18/2019

BALBOA.PRESS
A DIVISION OF HAY HOUSE

No More Strawberries

A Story About
Making Your
Dreams Come True

Kat Roberts

DEDICATION

This book is dedicated to my children. I love you all so very much. Thank you for being my greatest teachers.

Endless gratitude is due to all those that make my life joyful and smooth and made it possible for me to pursue this project: Ken, Brenda, Eliz, Rafael, Carlos... thank you! I love you all and I am grateful you are part of my life.

This is Elissa.

She lives with her Mom, Dad, two brothers and one sister. All her grandparents visit often, sometimes it feels like they live there too.

They live on a strawberry farm.

Strawberries grow in huge fields behind their house.

Every strawberry season, all her family work hard to grow and gather the delicious red berries.

They gather so many baskets of berries that their storage barn overflows.

The kitchen overflows.

The fridge overflows.

And sometimes there are even strawberries in random places all around the house.

For a few weeks each summer, Elissa's family use the strawberries to make strawberry jam.

And strawberry pies...

Strawberry ice cream...

Strawberry fruit bars...

Strawberry popsicles...

Strawberry everything!

Every day they all take turns selling strawberries at their market stand.

And every day, the strawberries sell out because customers love them so much.

Elissa's mother often says, "Wow! We are so blessed to have an abundance of strawberries!"

Elissa isn't too sure what that means, but she does know that there are just *too* many berries everywhere.

Everyone in her family loves strawberries.

They all love working on the strawberry farm.

They all love everything to do with strawberries.

Everyone is very happy.

Everyone except Elissa.

Because, Elissa doesn't like strawberries *at all*.

And this is a problem because no one in her family knows.

Elissa is too scared to tell them.

She thinks they will get mad at her.

Or worse, make fun of her for being different than them.

So, she keeps quiet.

She keeps quiet even though every day she has this strong feeling inside her that she is meant to do something that has *nothing* to do with strawberries.

The only time she can get a break from strawberries is when she's alone in her room or when she is asleep.

Sometimes she'll sit quietly in her room and imagine herself doing exactly what she wants to be doing. She is so happy that she can use her imagination to help her *feel* the feelings of what it would be like to be doing what she loves.

When she sleeps, Elissa can also go to the place she loves most. In her dreams is when she gets to spend time with the things that make her heart happy. When she wakes up, she feels excited and like maybe her dreams have finally come true.

But then she sees her strawberry pillows and curtains and remembers she is still in the same room, on the same strawberry farm.

One morning, just like many others, there was a bowl of strawberries waiting for her at breakfast.

And, she just couldn't hold it in anymore.

The voice inside her finally spoke up.

"NO MORE STRAWBERRIES!" she exclaimed.

Then, to her surprise, she said more.

"I don't like eating them! I don't want to be a strawberry farmer! I don't like that my room is all decorated in strawberries! I am just NOT a strawberry person!"

Everyone in her family was eating their breakfast at the table. They were all startled and looked up at her.

Elissa felt scared. She had never, ever told them about how much she didn't like strawberries.

But when Elissa looked more closely at their faces, no one looked mad, and no one was laughing at her.

She started to feel calmer and safer, but she still didn't know *what* anyone would say.

She hid her face in her hands.

Then she peeked through her fingers.

Her mom was kneeling in front of her. Her eyes were kind.

"Oh Elissa. It's OK. You don't need to like strawberries just because everyone else in our family does."

Elissa couldn't believe what she was hearing!

"I don't?" She asked hesitantly.

"No, you don't. Our dream doesn't have to be your dream." Her mother replied.

"What *do* you like?" Her father asked.

Elissa knew right away what her answer would be.

She had been waiting for this day for so long, she could hardly believe it was finally here.

"I LOVE WHALES! I love everything about them! I love learning about them! I want to decorate my room in everything whales! And I want to be a whale scientist and study whales and the ocean!"

Elissa went and did just that.

A NOTE TO THE READER

One day my daughter, who at the time was 7 years old, told me she felt different than the rest of her family because she didn't like jam and she thought we would be upset.

I sat down with her and explained that everyone has different likes and dislikes and we don't all have to be the same.

Around the same time, my older daughter, who at the time was 12, was going through the early phase of adolescence and I was beginning to sense a shift in her. I noticed that quite suddenly, all her childhood dreams, which had been so vivid and possible to her previously, were now appearing to be less attainable and she was beginning to lose that magical belief she had in them.

My mind and heart began to process these various dilemmas my children were in and I became inspired to write something that touched on these topics.

Only you get to decide what you like and what your dreams are!

Only you can decide if you keep the magic and belief in your life dreams alive!

I quickly found there are few children's books that talk about being authentic to oneself, about self-worth, self-advocacy, and the power of manifestation.

I believe that as children grow up, we should be encouraging them to keep the magic in their dreams alive...to keep believing in themselves and giving them the tools they need to manifest their dreams into reality.

The topic of manifestation is layered and rich in deep teachings and learning. But I have seen this be so simple and easy for children and they inherently possess this power! It is my deepest wish for children to keep that power within them and as they grow older for them not to forget that they can create their desired reality...with belief, love, focus, clear intentions and hard work.

Dream big. Be true. Be brave. Believe. Create. Be grateful.

Printed in the United States
By Bookmasters